blue
rider
press

# I FEEL BAD

## All Day. Every Day. About Everything.

### ORLI AUSLANDER

BLUE RIDER PRESS

NEW YORK

blue
rider
press

An imprint of Penguin Random House LLC
375 Hudson Street
New York, New York 10014

# FOR SHAL

FOR YOUR LOVE, YOUR LAUGHTER,
YOUR HERESY, YOUR INSPIRATION,
YOUR ENCOURAGEMENT FROM DAY ONE,
FOR PUTTING UP WITH MY SHIT,
BUT MOSTLY, FOR BEING SO
THOROUGHLY "OTHER"

## Introduction

**H**ave you ever found yourself inviting someone you hate over to dinner simply because you feel bad that they invited you to a party you didn't want to go to in the first place but you went because you felt bad because their dog died the month before? Yes, it was a nasty little yappy bastard who'd nipped you a number of times, but it was abused during puppyhood so you felt bad for that too. If some of this sounds familiar, then unfortunately you and I have something in common: we feel bad. A lot.

Given that I am both female and Jewish, feeling bad was a ubiquitous part of growing up. I was quite used to it and didn't really give it much thought. After all, I was born and raised in the United Kingdom, where we apologize incessantly for everything except raping and pillaging other countries. For a long time I chalked it up to having Middle Eastern parents. For the uninitiated, let me get you up to speed.

But then I noticed that feeling bad isn't unique to Brits or Middle Easterners or females or Jews. Men feel bad. Catholics feel bad; so do Mormons. Even the bloody Buddhists feel bad . . . why else would they need to spend so many hours meditating?

Years later I moved from London to New York, and after having a baby in my mid-thirties, I felt bad that I'd waited so long; I began to notice that I felt bad all day, every day, about everything. At first I thought it was the raging hormones. But this didn't explain why I was carrying around enough guilt for all the world's murderers, rapists, and child molesters.

Twenty years of therapy provided a few plausible reasons.

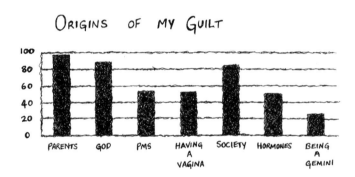

ORIGINS OF MY GUILT

But in my state of postpartum lunacy, I'd stopped giving a shit about why I felt bad. I just needed to alleviate some of the guilt.

So, looking for a way to defuse these feelings, I began keeping a tiny black I Feel Bad notebook around to jot down the times I felt bad—mostly as an experiment to see how many times a day the bad feelings arose (thank you, Cognitive Behavioral Therapy). I very quickly realized that the "few" times a day was actually all the time. No matter what I was doing—breast-feeding, taking the new sprog to the doctor, walking the dog—my derogatory, critical, bitchy self would start pointing out what

I was doing wrong (everything) and why I was such a shitty person. The list grew longer and longer and longer.

Then something interesting happened: the more I pulled out my notebook, the louder became my long-dormant sweet and tender rational side.

I started to illustrate some of the I Feel Bads on my list, hoping to laugh at myself, and the sense of relief during the forty-five minutes a day of drawing became a much-needed though brief escape from the prison of my guilt-drenched brain.

DON'T BE SUCH A FUCKING IDIOT! YOU CAN'T BE THAT BAD A PERSON ALL THE TIME. TWIT!

A few months later I was asked to show my work at a local gallery. I was ambivalent. The work is very personal and I'd never imagined other people looking at it; showing your personal bits is not the Middle Eastern way.

I agreed to do the show and was surprised by the reactions from viewers. People, young and old, male and female, expressed appreciation, horror, tears, laughter, disgust, and often outrage, but mainly commiseration. Strangers began to share their own experiences of feeling bad, and for me this felt like validation. Neurotics love company.

So here it is, a collection of some of the many reasons I feel bad and how they affect me in everyday life. Undoubtedly they come from being a woman, a Brit, a Jew, a Middle Easterner, a Gemini, but mostly they come from being hopelessly human.

If, like me, you waste a lot of time feeling bad, I hope this collection makes you laugh. If not, no doubt I'll feel bad.

I FEEL BAD

I FEEL BAD #1

I DO NOT WANT TO LOOK LIKE MY MOTHER.

I FEEL BAD #2

I HIDE FROM MY KIDS
IN MY OWN HOUSE.

I FEEL BAD #3

I INSIST IT'S NOT PMS.

I FEEL BAD #4

I TRANSFER MY FEARS.

I FEEL BAD #5

I SAY NO.

I FEEL BAD #6

I SAY YES.

I FEEL BAD #7

I HAVE BAGGAGE.

I FEEL BAD #8

SOMETIMES I REALLY HATE MY VAGINA.

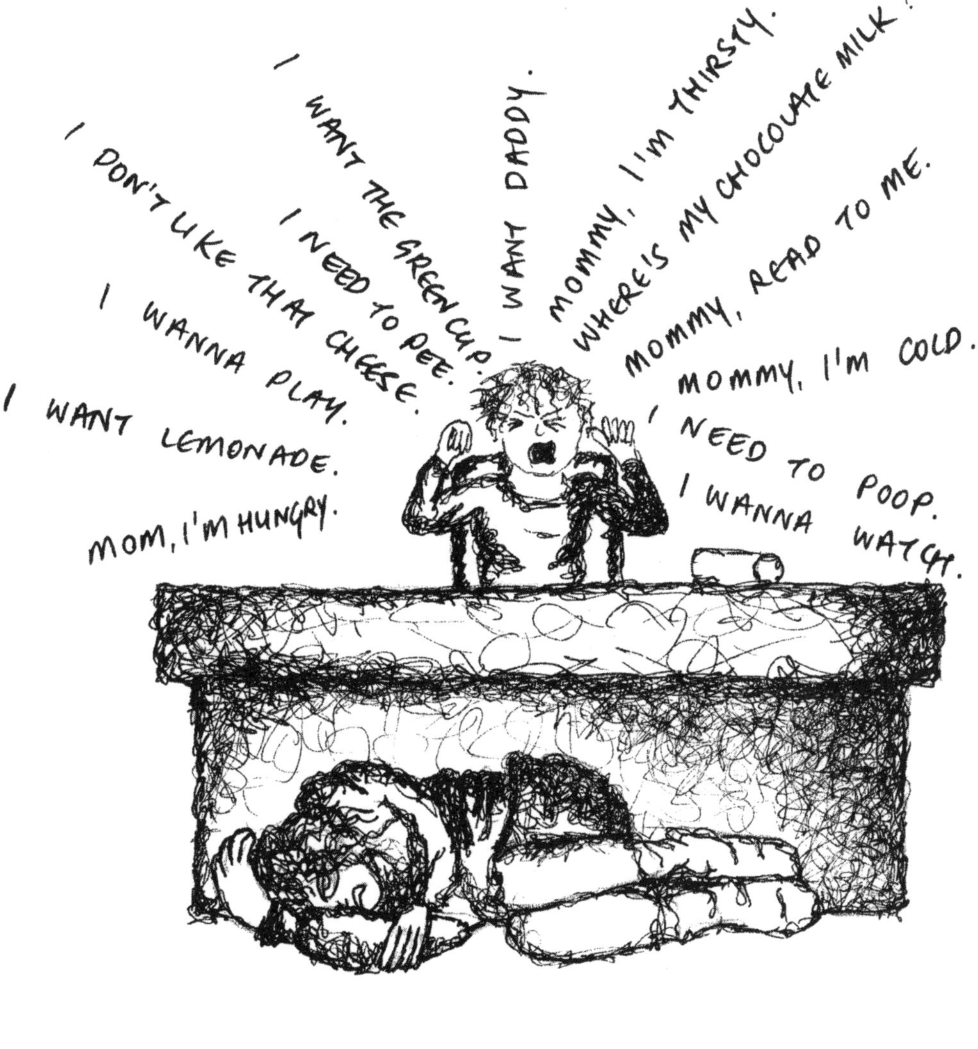
I WANT THE GREEN CUP.
I WANT DADDY.
MOMMY, I'M THIRSTY.
WHERE'S MY CHOCOLATE MILK?
I DON'T LIKE THAT CHEESE.
I NEED TO PEE.
MOMMY, READ TO ME.
I WANNA PLAY.
I WANT LEMONADE.
MOMMY, I'M COLD.
I NEED TO POOP.
I WANNA WATCH.
MOM, I'M HUNGRY.

I FEEL BAD #9

SOMETIMES I JUST DON'T GIVE A SHIT.

...THEN THE CLONE TROOPERS INVADED PLANET KASHYYYK AND DELTA SQUAD INFILTRATED A TRANDOSHAN MERCENARY CAMP TO RESCUE A WOOKIEE AND THEY GOT ALL THESE SECRETS ABOUT THE CONFEDERACY'S ALLIANCE WITH THE MERCENARIES AND THEN THE COMMANDOS HAD TO FIND TARFFUL BUT THEN SEV WAS ATTACKED AND THE SQUAD LOST CONTACT WITH HIM SO THEY WANTED TO LOOK FOR HIM BUT YODA SAID, "NO."

I FEEL BAD #10

I SHUT MY MOTHER OUT.

I FEEL BAD # 11

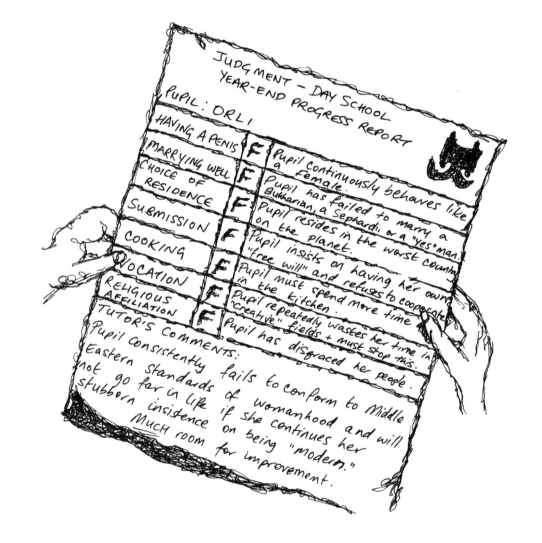

JUDGMENT — DAY SCHOOL
YEAR-END PROGRESS REPORT

PUPIL: ORLI

| | | |
|---|---|---|
| HAVING A PENIS | F | Pupil continuously behaves like a female. |
| MARRYING WELL | F | Pupil has failed to marry a Bukharian, a Sephardi, or a "yes-man." |
| CHOICE OF RESIDENCE | F | Pupil resides in the worst country on the planet. |
| SUBMISSION | F | Pupil insists on having her own "free will" and refuses to cooperate. |
| COOKING | F | Pupil must spend more time in the kitchen. |
| VOCATION | F | Pupil repeatedly wastes her time in "creative" fields + must stop this. |
| RELIGIOUS AFFILIATION | F | Pupil has disgraced her people. |

TUTOR'S COMMENTS:
Pupil consistently fails to conform to Middle Eastern standards of womanhood and will not go far in life if she continues her stubborn insistence on being "modern." MUCH room for improvement.

I FAILED MY FATHER.

I FEEL BAD #12

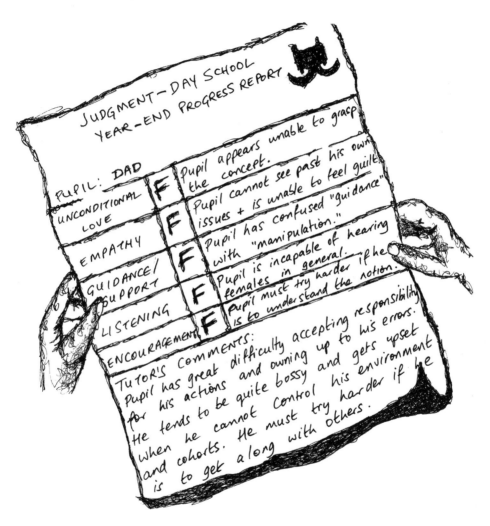

MY FATHER FAILED ME.

I FEEL BAD #13

I NEED SOMEONE TO BLAME.

I FEEL BAD #14

I LIKE VODKA.

I FEEL BAD #15

SOMETIMES I WANT TO GAG MY BABY.

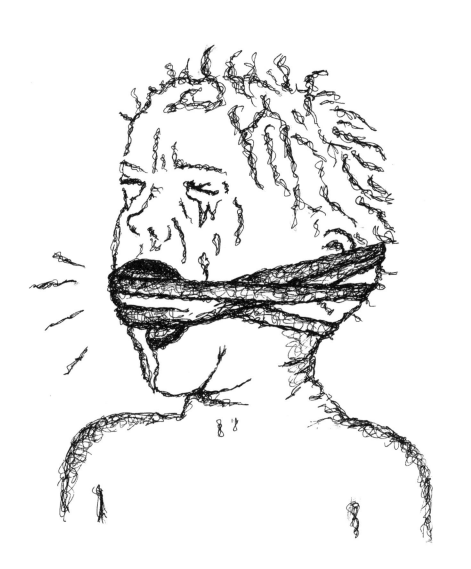

I FEEL BAD #16

I'M VENGEFUL.

THE WASP THAT STUNG MY SON.

LET THIS SERVE AS A WARNING
TO ANY OTHER MOTHER FUCKERS
WHO WANT TO TRY HURTING ONE
OF MY BOYS.

I FEEL BAD # 17

I CAN'T EXPLAIN EVERYTHING.

I FEEL BAD #18

I BUY MY KIDS TOO MANY TOYS.

I FEEL BAD #19

I'M SURE THE STUFF I BUY IS MADE
BY ENSLAVED CHILDREN, BUT I BUY
IT ANYWAY.

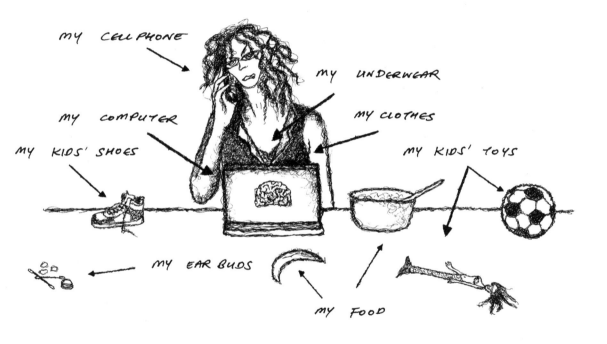

I FEEL BAD #20

I DON'T WANT TO KNOW.

CANCER

MISSING
Milk
WITH
ADDED
WHATEVER
GIRL/BOY
LAST SEEN:
FUCK KNOWS

CRIME SCENE DO NOT CROSS

I FEEL BAD #21

I'M DESTROYING THE PLANET.

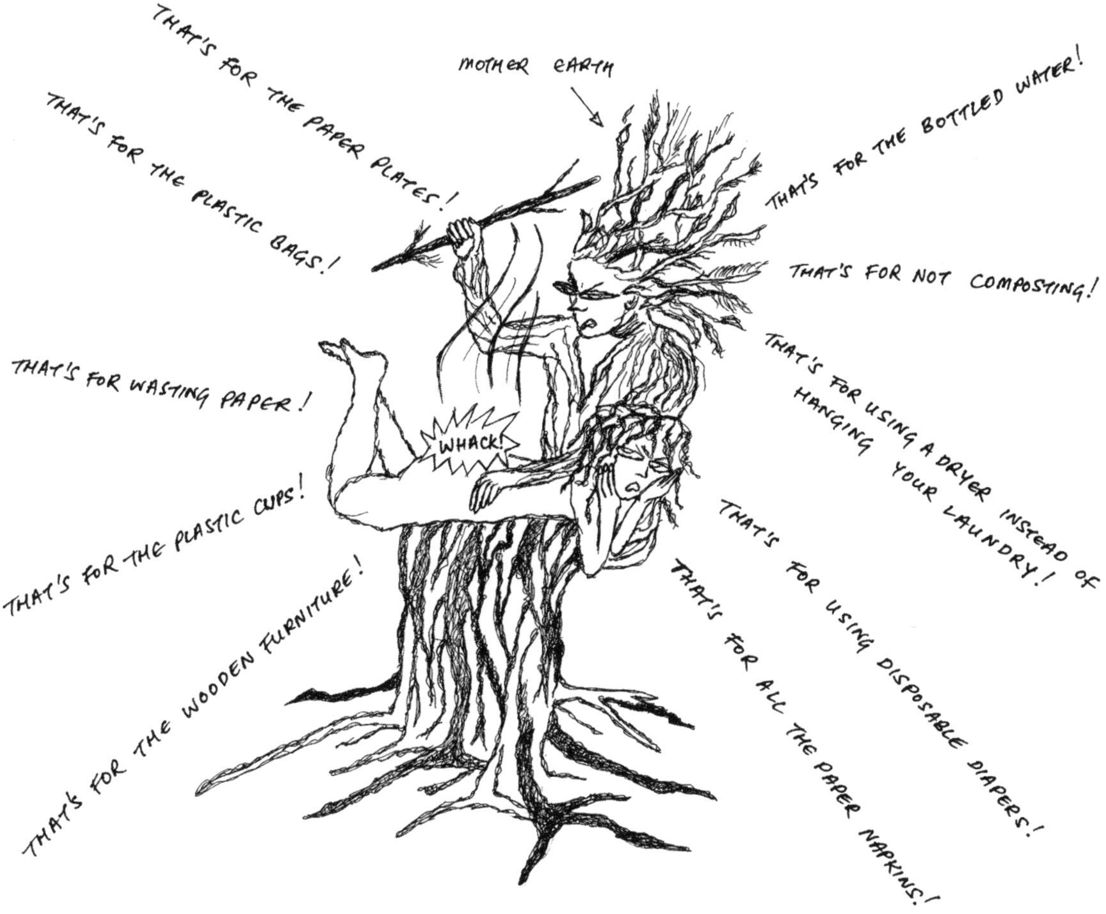
MOTHER EARTH
THAT'S FOR THE PAPER PLATES!
THAT'S FOR THE PLASTIC BAGS!
THAT'S FOR WASTING PAPER!
THAT'S FOR THE PLASTIC CUPS!
THAT'S FOR THE WOODEN FURNITURE!
THAT'S FOR THE BOTTLED WATER!
THAT'S FOR NOT COMPOSTING!
THAT'S FOR USING A DRYER INSTEAD OF HANGING YOUR LAUNDRY!
THAT'S FOR USING DISPOSABLE DIAPERS!
THAT'S FOR ALL THE PAPER NAPKINS!
WHACK!

I FEEL BAD #22

I DIDN'Y BREASTFEED LONG ENOUGH.

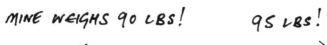

I FEEL BAD #23

I'M COMPETITIVE.

# I FEEL BAD #24

# I DON'T SHARE.

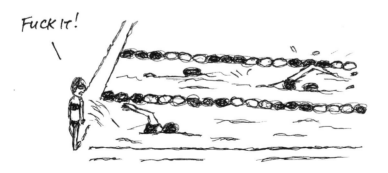

I FEEL BAD #25

I CUM MORE.

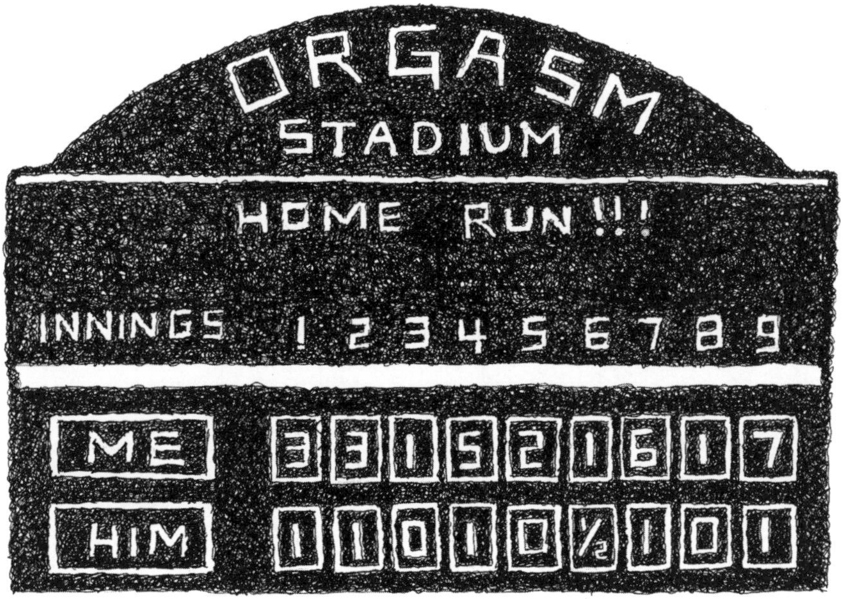
ORGASM
STADIUM
HOME RUN!!!
INNINGS 1 2 3 4 5 6 7 8 9
ME 3 3 1 5 2 1 6 1 7
HIM 1 1 0 1 0 ½ 1 0 1

# I FEEL BAD #26

... THAT'S SUCH BOLLOCKS. I'M NOT
LATE "EVERY" TIME, JUST SOME TIMES,
BUT THEY KNOW WE'RE GOING TO BE
LATE. EVERYONE'S AT LEAST 10 MINUTES
LATE TO RESTAURANTS, SO IF THEY'RE
EXPECTING US TO BE LATE, IT'S NOT
REALLY "HOLDING" THE TABLE FOR US
AND WE'RE BASICALLY ON TIME, SINCE
NO ONE'S REALLY ON TIME AND IT'S
NOT LIKE ANYONE'S STANDING THERE
DEMANDING THE TABLE JUST 'CAUSE
WE'RE A FEW MINUTES LATE, AND
ANYWAY WE WERE ONLY 20 MINUTES
LATE THIS TIME AND I DID CALL TO
SAY WE'D BE LATE, PLUS WE'RE
THERE EVERY BLOODY WEEK.
YOU THINK THEY DON'T KNOW WE'RE
GOING TO BE A BIT LATE?

# I'M ARGUMENTATIVE.

# I FEEL BAD #27

I TAKE PROZAC - ONLY 30 MG A <u>WEEK</u> - AND YET,
I FEEL LIKE A WEAK, PATHETIC LOSER WHO
CAN'T FUNCTION WITHOUT "RUNNING FOR THE
SHELTER" OF MY "MOTHER'S LITTLE HELPER,"
AND FUCK THAT FUCKING JUDGMENTAL SONG,
WRITTEN BY TWO CLUELESS, HYPOCRITICAL
JUNKIES, MAY THEY BOTH GROW A PAIR OF
OVARIES AND DROWN IN A VAT OF
TESTOSTERONE... KNIGHTHOOD, MY ASS!

# I FEEL BAD #28

I HATE PEOPLE I'VE NEVER MET.

I FEEL BAD  #29

I ENCOURAGED MY BROTHER TO FIND GOD.

I FEEL BAD   # 30

I'M SELF-HATING.

I FEEL BAD # 31

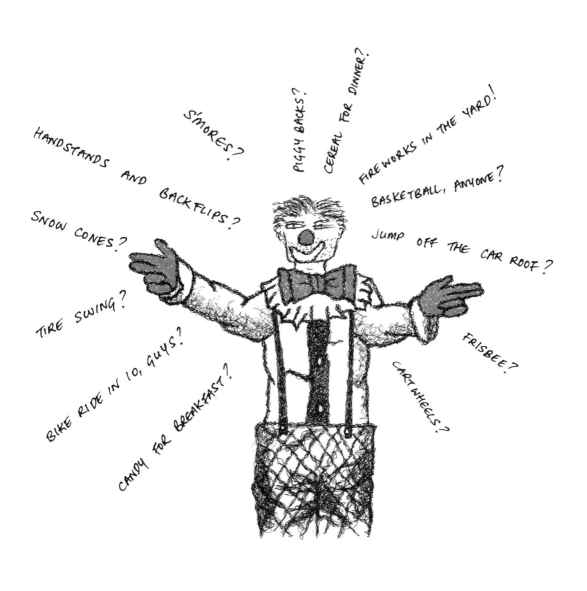

MY HUSBAND'S ALWAYS THE FUN ONE.

I FEEL BAD # 32

I DON'T GIVE ENOUGH.

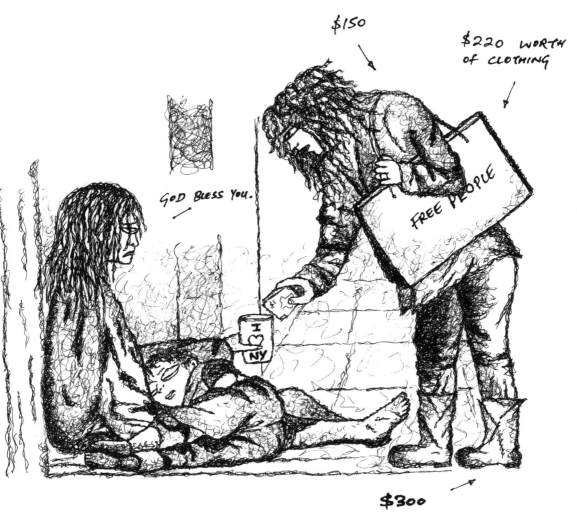

I FEEL BAD #33

MY KIDS BARELY KNOW THEY'RE JEWISH.

# I FEEL BAD   #34

I DON'T WANT TO HEAR MY FATHER'S
OPINIONS ON BIRTH CONTROL AND THE
"RIGHT" AGE TO HAVE BABIES AND THE
BEST COUNTRY TO RAISE CHILDREN IN OR
HIS OPINIONS ON WHY LONDON IS SO
MUCH BETTER THAN NEW YORK OR
ON CRIME STATISTICS IN AMERICA
VERSUS ENGLAND OR ON WHY IT'S THE
JOB OF A WOMAN TO HAVE CHILDREN
OR ON WHO GOD MADE AND WHY
OR ON HOW SPECIAL JEWS ARE
OR ON WHY ISRAELIS ARE SOOOOO
CLEVER OR ON WHY PRAYER REALLY
WORKS AND HOW IT'S BEEN SCIENTIFICALLY
PROVEN.

I FEEL BAD # 35

I LET MY SIX-YEAR-OLD
LISTEN TO EMINEM.

I FEEL BAD # 36

I COULDN'T SAVE MY SON'S
FAVORITE TOY FROM THE DOG.

# I FEEL BAD #37

SOMETIMES, BEING A MUM MAKES ME
WANT TO GET SOME SHITTY JOB JUST
SO I CAN SAY I'M BEING PAID FOR
MY TIME, WHICH REMINDS ME THAT
MY SELF-WORTH IS DEPENDENT UPON
A SALARY.

... AND SIGN MY PERMISSION SLIP AND HERE'S A
LETTER ABOUT LICE AND TOMORROW'S FIELD DAY
I HAVE TO WEAR RED AND I NEED MONEY FOR
PIZZA AND TUESDAY'S THE BELT TEST — YOU
HAVE TO COME AND YOU HAVE TO MAKE A
WIZARD COSTUME FOR DRESS REHEARSAL ON
THURSDAY AND I HAVE TO BRING MY LIBRARY
BOOKS BY TOMORROW AND DO WE HAVE A
HEATER FOR THE SCIENCE FAIR? AND I NEED
NEW BASKETBALL SNEAKERS AND PLEASE
PLEASE PLEASE COME TO THE POTLUCK AND
THE FILM FESTIVAL AND THE PIANO RECITAL
AND COMMUNITY DAY AND THE PARENT
LUNCH AND THE AUCTION AND THE CLOTHING
SWAP AND THE SPORTS DINNER AND THE...

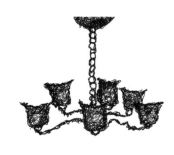

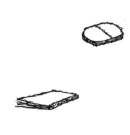

I FEEL BAD # 38

I GET SICK OF BEING NEEDED.

I FEEL BAD # 39

I'M A HYPOCRITE.

I FEEL BAD # 40

I HAD THE VET RIP OUT MY DOG'S
UTERUS AND OVARIES AND SHE'S
BEEN INCONTINENT EVER SINCE.

I FEEL BAD #41

I EAT MEAT.

I FEEL BAD # 42

I LIE TO MY KIDS.

I FEEL BAD # 43

I DON'T LIE TO MY KIDS.

I FEEL BAD # 44

I MAKE RULES.

NO MORE SUGAR!

NO MORE LATE NIGHTS!

NO MORE GODDAMN SPORTS!

NO MORE BOOZE!

NO MORE FUCKING DOGS!

NO MORE FUCKING!

NO MORE SPROGS!

NO MORE BLOODY SCREENS!

NO MORE RULES!

I FEEL BAD #45

I DON'T DO ANAL.

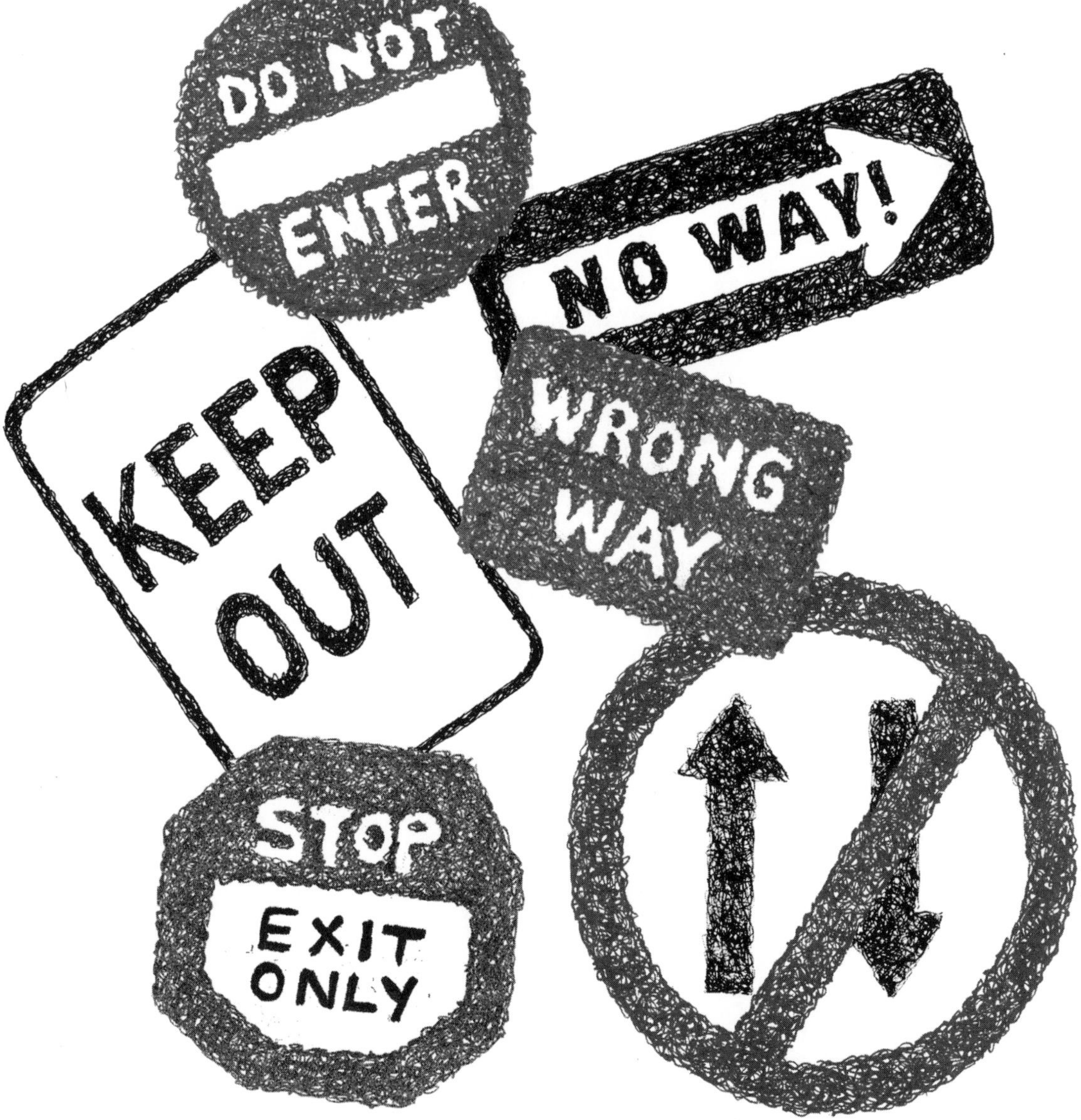
DO NOT
ENTER
NO WAY!
KEEP
OUT
WRONG
WAY
STOP
EXIT
ONLY

I FEEL BAD #46

I GET DEFENSIVE.

I FEEL BAD #47

EVERYONE'S   A SUSPECT.

WHAT MEDS?

I NEED MEDS? WHAT

WHAT

WHY ARE YOU CALLING?

D'YOU GO TO MY DOG?

ORGANIC? SAYS WHO?

WHERE'S MY CHANGE?

D'YOU TAKE MY GOGGLES?

YOU LOOKING AT ME?

HOW LONG ARE YOU GONNA BE?

WHAT'S IN THAT BUG SPRAY?

WHERE'S MY NAPKIN?

WHO TOOK MY KEYS?

WHO ATE MY CHOCOLATE?

WHAT'S WITH THE QUESTIONS?

WHAT D'YOU PUT IN THOSE CUPCAKES?

YOU FUCKING WITH ME?

WHO MOVED MY BAG?

WHERE ARE MY TAMPONS?

WHERE'S THE CONTRACT?

WHY DOES MY SON NEED AN X-RAY?

WHO WANTS TO KNOW?

WHO USED MY PHONE?

WHY SHOULD I SIGN IT?

# I FEEL BAD #48

I PRESSURE MY SON TO STOP
SUCKING HIS THUMB EVEN THOUGH I,
IN MY MID-FORTIES, STILL HAVE
ANXIOUS BOUTS OF PICKING MY
LIPS TILL THEY BLEED, AN ORAL
FIXATION THAT BEGAN WHEN I WAS
TRYING TO STOP SUCKING MY
OWN THUMB WHEN I WAS HIS AGE.

I FEEL BAD # 49

I SAY THE WRONG THING.

I FEEL BAD #50

I KILL.

1,252 MOSQUITOS

2 BUTTERFLIES

48,000 LICE

6 MICE

4 CHIPMUNKS

3 SQUIRRELS

2000 — 2005

BAMBI    MAMA

2 DEER

4 BIRDS

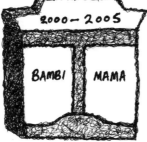

FRIED LIES HERE

1 TURTLE

16 WASPS

1 GRASSHOPPER

3 BATS

402 FLIES

1 BEAVER

SALLY  LILLY  MANNY  DEE DEE  JILL

5 SALAMANDERS

2 RABBITS

I FEEL BAD #51

MY CYNICISM HAS RUBBED OFF.

I FEEL BAD #52

I USE STUPID CLICHÉS.

I FEEL BAD #53

I'M IRRESPONSIBLE.

# I FEEL BAD #54

I DON'T PICK UP THE OLD HITCHHIKER
WITH THE BUM LEG, EVEN THOUGH NO ONE'S
GOING TO DIE IF MY FIRST GRADER IS
FIVE MINUTES LATE FOR SCHOOL, AND BESIDES,
THE OLD GEEZER'S NOT GOING TO HURT ME
OR MY KIDS AND THEN HOBBLE AWAY ON
HIS WALKING STICK, IS HE?

I FEEL BAD #55

I'M HIGH MAINTENANCE.

I FEEL BAD #56

I RUSH.

UICK... DENTIST!

MOVE IT!
SCHOOL!

HURRY UP!... BUS!

COME ON!
DINNER!

LET'S GO!
NAP!

MAKE IT SNAPPY!
CLEANUP TIME!

BED!...NOW!

FASTER!
BURY ME!

I FEEL BAD #57

I BAD-MOUTH PEOPLE
IN FRONT OF MY KIDS.

I FEEL BAD #58

I'M JUDGMENTAL.

GO PLAY,
YOU LIKE HER!

I HATE HER!

STOP EATING DIRT!

SON'S A DIMWIT

PARENTS KEPT THEIR KID
BEHIND TO GIVE HIM AN
ADVANTAGE.

HELICOPTER MUM

PARENTS ARE FUCKING CHEATS

FAKE LIPS

FAKE TITS

FAKE BUM

INSECURE SUCKER

FUCKING TRUSTAFARIAN

POSING AS A HIPPIE

SHITTY FATHER

USERS

TERRIFIED OF
HIS BRAT

SOOOOOOOO JUDGMENTAL

MONEY-GRUBBING
SLAPPER

MIDLIFE CRISIS,
CRADLE-SNATCHING
SHALLOW TWAT

I WANT IT!
I WANT IT!
I WANT IT!

I FEEL BAD #59

I'M POLITE WHEN I SHOULD BE RUDE.

I FEEL BAD #60

I'M RUDE WHEN I SHOULD BE POLITE.

HOW COULD YOU POSSIBLY KNOW WHAT I'M GOING THROUGH?
DO YOU HAVE A FUCKING VAGINA? NO! DO YOU HAVE A
UTERUS? DON'T LOOK AT ME LIKE THAT! LIKE YOU'RE
SO FUCKING SUPERIOR! I KNOW WHAT YOU'RE THINKING!
GO ON! SAY IT! YOU SAY THE SAME SHIT OVER AND
OVER AGAIN! YOU THINK I DON'T KNOW I'M FUCKING
HORMONAL? THE MEDS DO FUCK ALL! THEY'RE USELESS!
I DON'T KNOW WHY I KEEP COMING HERE! WASTE OF
FUCKING TIME! TWENTY YEARS DOWN THE FUCKING TOILET!

I FEEL BAD #61

I HATE OTHER PEOPLE'S CHILDREN.

I FEEL BAD # 62

I HIDE MY FAVORITE CHOCOLATES.

I FEEL BAD # 63

I MAKE HIM WASH THE DILDOS.

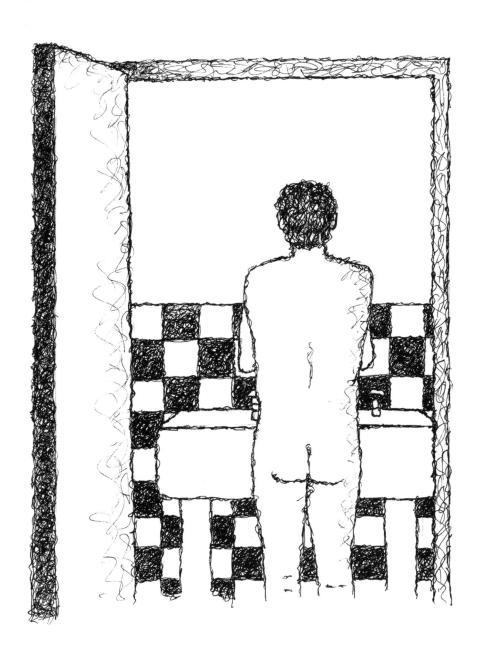

I FEEL BAD #64

I HAVE MOODS.

8:00

 HOORAY!

8:30

 !

8:01

 SHIT!

8:27

YESSS!

8:03

 YIPPEE!

8:23

NOOOOO!

8:06

 I'LL KILL HIM!

8:22

SWEEEET!

8:10

 YAHOOOO!

8:19

FUCK IT!

8:11

 KILL ME NOW!

8:15

WOO-HOO!

I FEEL BAD #65

I DITCHED MY BROTHER'S WEDDING.

R.S.V.P.

Before Jan. 12th 2006

ORLI

will **NOT** attend.

Please indicate number of persons for each entrée

O  Chicken entrée

O  Fish entrée

I FEEL BAD #66

I CURSE TOO FUCKING MUCH.

I FEEL BAD # 67

I REFUSE TO ASK FOR HELP,
THEN I EXPLODE BECAUSE
NO ONE HELPS.

I FEEL BAD #68

I WANT TO CONTROL
EVERYTHING AND EVERYONE.

TOO MUCH SUGAR!

TOO MUCH PORN!

TOO MUCH LIFE!

TOO MUCH SPENDING!

American TOO MANY DELAYS!

TOO MANY SNOW DAYS!

WOODSTOCK DAY SCHOOL
WELCOME

MORE VEGGIES!

TOO LONG TO CUM!

I DON'T GO TO THERAPY ENOUGH.

# I FEEL BAD #70

MAYBE THE SELF-FLAGELLATION'S JUST A RUDIMENTARY
INSTINCT INSTILLED BY MY PARENTS AND I'M SIMPLY
PROJECTING MY ANGER ONTO YOU... A SORT OF
REGRESSION, YOU COULD SAY, WHICH ALWAYS LEADS
TO MY UNWILLINGNESS TO EXPRESS MYSELF
HONESTLY AND THEN I JUST SUBCONSCIOUSLY TRANSFER...

# I GO TO THERAPY TOO MUCH.

I FEEL BAD #71

I LOVE THE BABYSITTER.

I FEEL BAD #72

I ONLY EAT THE PIECRUST.

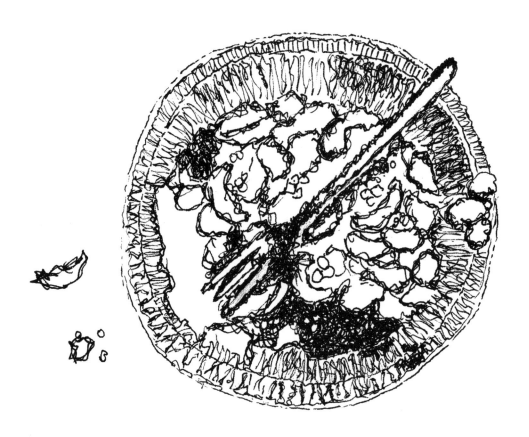

I FEEL BAD #73

I PAY SOMEONE TO CLEAN UP MY SHIT.

I FEEL BAD # 74

I ASSUME ALL MEN ARE RAPISTS.

I FEEL BAD # 75

I CANNOT SAVE MY PARENTS.

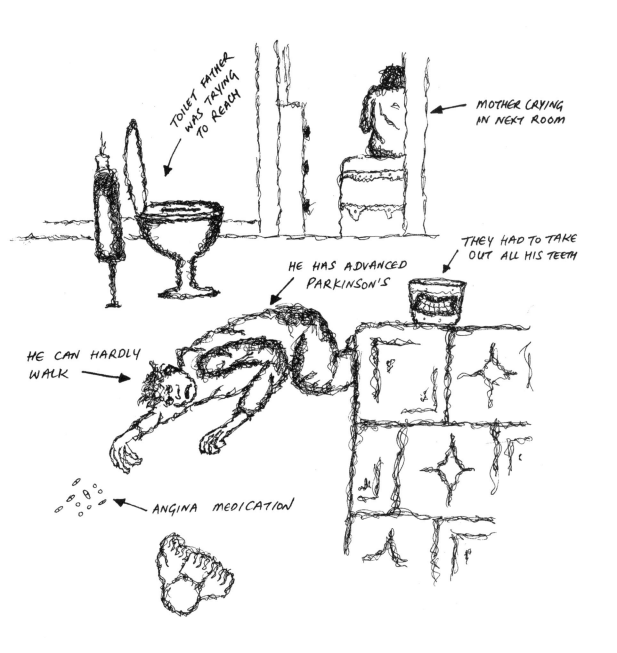

I FEEL BAD # 76

MY BROTHER LOVES GOD MORE THAN ME.

I FEEL BAD #77

I'M BITCHY.

I SAID "UNSALTED," AND IT'S NOT EVEN ORGANIC.

I FEEL BAD #78

I'M ALWAYS LATE FOR PRESCHOOL.

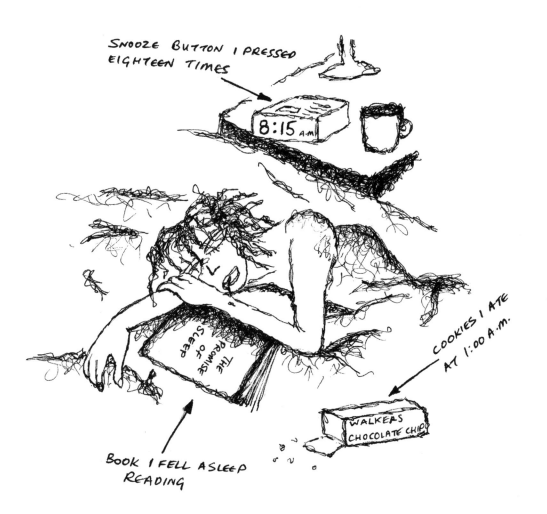

SNOOZE BUTTON I PRESSED
EIGHTEEN TIMES

8:15 A.M

COOKIES I ATE
AT 1:00 A.M.

WALKERS
CHOCOLATE CHIP

THE PROMISE OF SLEEP

BOOK I FELL ASLEEP
READING

I FEEL BAD # 79

I DON'T LET MY KIDS EAT POISON.

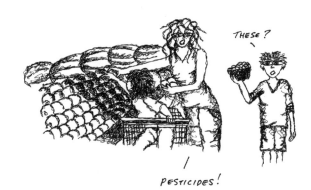

I FEEL BAD   # 80

I LET MY KIDS EAT POISON.

YAAAY!
CEREAL FOR DINNER.

YAY!
DEEP FRIED OREOS.

YAY!
CORN DOGS.

I FEEL BAD #81

I CHUCKED HIS HALLOWEEN CANDY...
AND LIED ABOUT IT.

I FEEL BAD # 82

I WANT TO MAKE THE BIRTHDAY CAKE.

I FEEL BAD #83

I DON'T WANT TO MAKE
THE FUCKING BIRTHDAY CAKE.

... AND I WANT ARIEL ON IT AND RAPUNZEL AND
MULAN AND DOROTHY TOO AND I WANT CINDERELLA
ON IT AND MOTHER GOTHEL AND ANNA AND ELSA
AND THE WICKED WITCH OF THE WEST AND THE
GOOD WITCH TOO AND I WANT TINTIN ON IT AND
SNOWY AND CAPTAIN HADDOCK AS WELL AND
I WANT HARRY POTTER ON IT AND LUNA LOVEGOOD
'CAUSE SHE'S AWESOME AND FLYNNY AND TASHA
AND IT HAS TO BE GLUTEN FREE FOR PAIX
AND IT HAS TO HAVE BUTTERFLIES ON IT AND
LADYBUGS 'CAUSE ILA LOVES LADYBUGS AND
IT HAS TO HAVE ...

I FEEL BAD #84

I TAKE THINGS PERSONALLY.

I FEEL BAD #85

I MISS IMPORTANT MOMENTS.

I FEEL BAD # 86

I'VE SPENT HIS COLLEGE SAVINGS
ON SHIT I DON'T NEED.

I FEEL BAD #87

I NAG.

I FEEL BAD # 88

I UNDERESTIMATE MY CHILDREN.

I'LL BET SHE HAS A
CRUSH ON YOU TOO.

MOM, I KNOW YOU'RE
TRYING TO MAKE ME
FEEL GOOD, BUT YOU'RE
JUST GIVING ME
FALSE HOPE.

# I FEEL BAD # 89

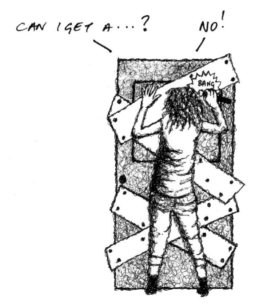

I'M OVERPROTECTIVE.

I FEEL BAD #90

I ENVY.

THEIR FUCKING FRIENDSHIP.

HIS FUCKING MINI.

HER FUCKING JOIE DE VIVRE.

HI! IS MY KID
AT YOUR HOUSE?

HER FUCKING YOUTH.

HER FUCKING
CAREFREE ATTITUDE.

I'M A HUGE FAN.

I LOVE YOU, MA!

THEIR FUCKING CLOSENESS.

HER FUCKING TRUST FUND.

HIS FUCKING CAREER.

I FEEL BAD #91

I KILL THE MOOD.

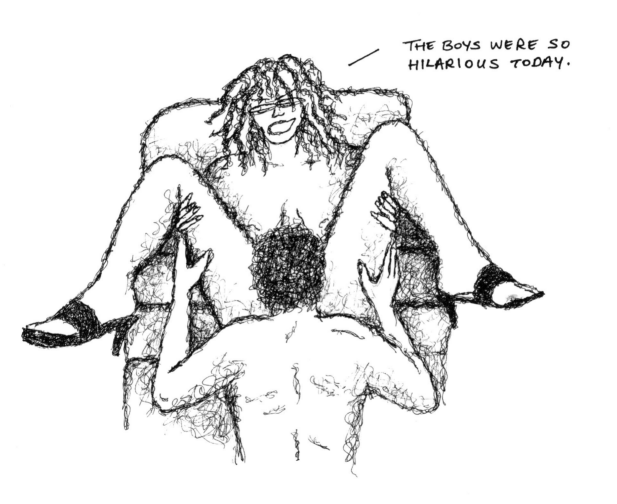

I FEEL BAD # 92

I KEEP DOMESTIC SCORE.

WHAT AM I, THE RESIDENT FUCKING CHEF?
I'VE MADE DINNER EVERY NIGHT, PLUS
THREE LOADS OF FUCKING LAUNDRY.
I PACKED THE LUNCHES, DID FOUR
LOTS OF FOOD SHOPPING, AND TOOK
THE DOGS TO THE VET. SO WHAT
IF HE DID THE FUCKING YARD WORK
AND FED THE DOGS AND TOOK OUT
THE GARBAGE? THAT SHIT'S EASY!

I FEEL BAD #93

I LIKE MY POT-INFUSED BATHS.

I FEEL BAD # 94

I USE SCREENS TO BUY TIME.

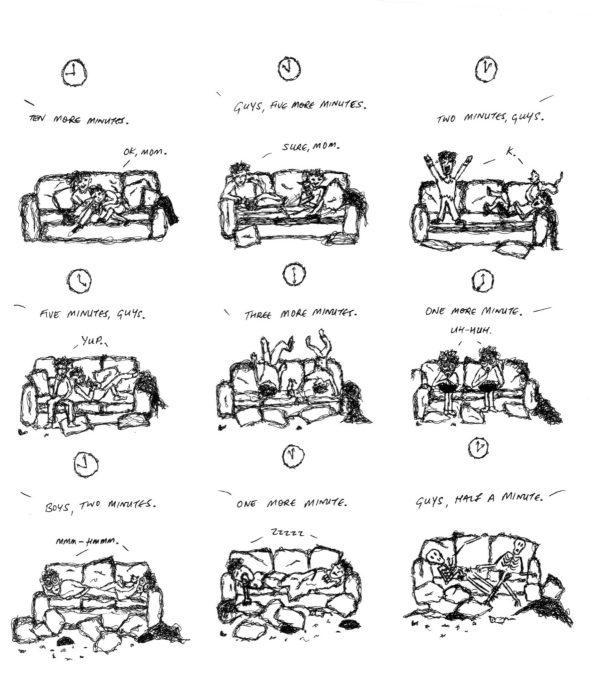

I FEEL BAD #95

I BINGE IN SECRET.

I FEEL BAD # 97

MY HUSBAND
IS AT THE MERCY
OF MY HORMONES.

12 P.M.

1:30 P.M.

4 P.M.

6:30 P.M.

8 P.M.

8:01 P.M.

I FEEL BAD #98

I KICK THE DOGS OFF THE BED.

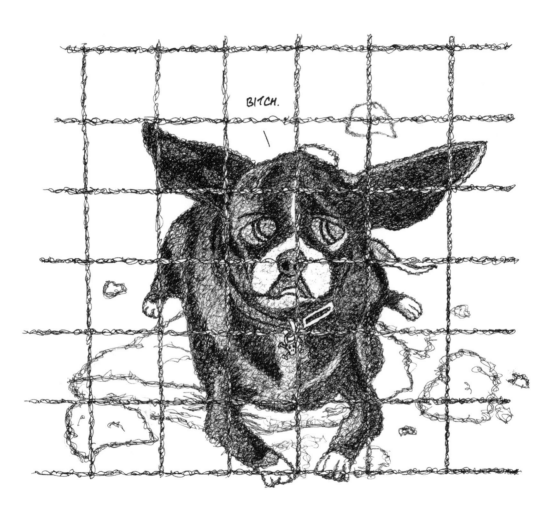

I FEEL BAD #99

I DON'T WEAR THE LINGERIE
MY HUSBAND BUYS ME.

I FEEL BAD # 100

ALL DAY, EVERY DAY, FOR EVERYfuckingTHING.

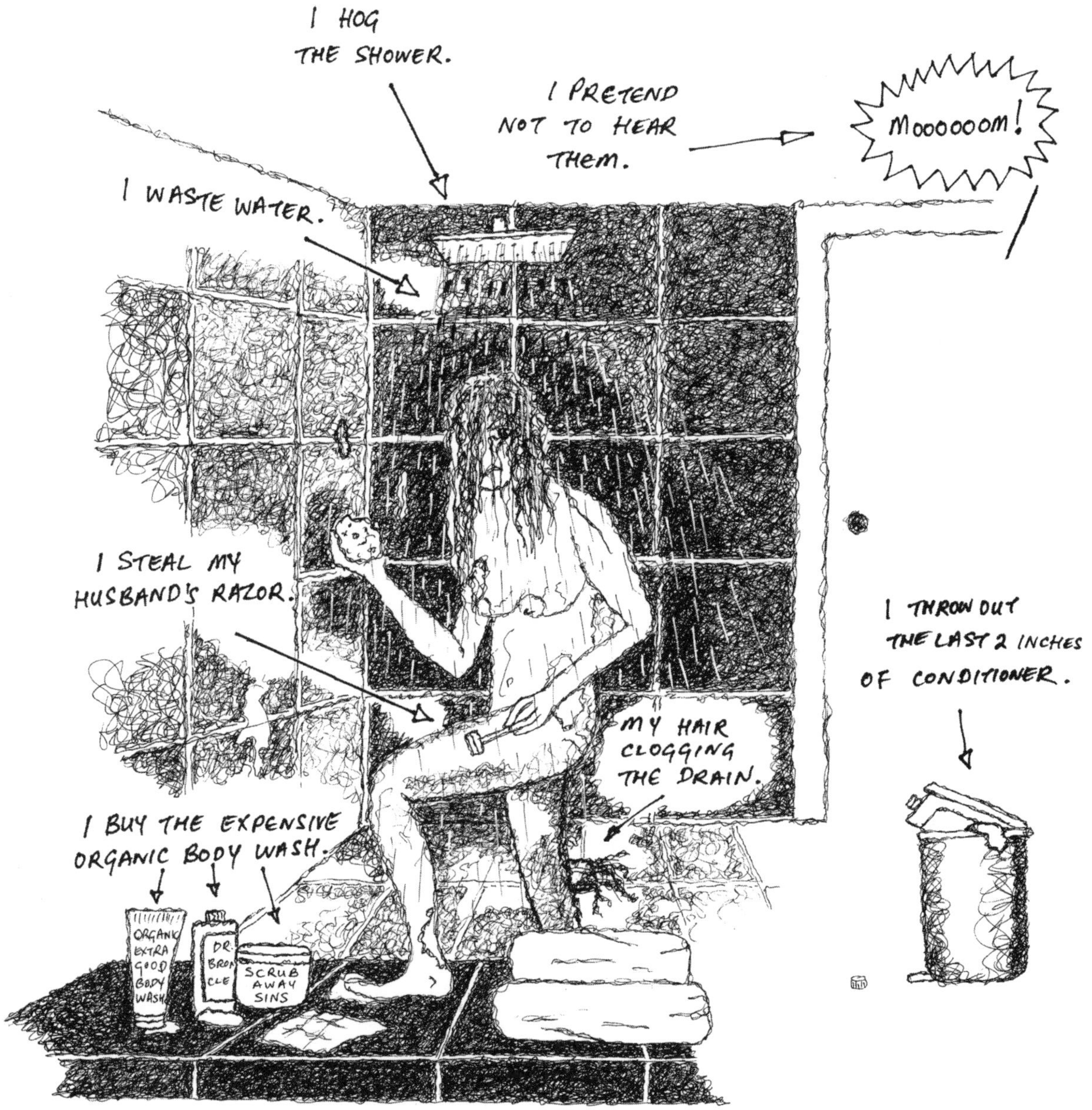
I HOG THE SHOWER.
I PRETEND NOT TO HEAR THEM.
Moooooom!
I WASTE WATER.
I STEAL MY HUSBAND'S RAZOR.
I THROW OUT THE LAST 2 INCHES OF CONDITIONER.
MY HAIR CLOGGING THE DRAIN.
I BUY THE EXPENSIVE ORGANIC BODY WASH.
ORGANIC EXTRA GOOD BODY WASH
SCRUB AWAY SINS

# I FEEL BAD #101

I HAVE DRAGGED THE FOLLOWING GENEROUS PEOPLE
INTO MY MORASS OF GUILT:

SHALOM, PAIX, AND LUX
DAVID ROSENTHAL
SARAH HOCHMAN
MEREDITH KAFFEL SIMONOFF
GEOFF KLOSKE
JODY HOTCHKISS
IKE HERSCHKOPF
SNEHA KEPADIA
AILEEN BOYLE
BRIAN ULICKY
KAYLEIGH GEORGE
JASON BOOHER
TEREZIA CICELOVA


THANK YOU ALL, FROM THE BOTTOM
OF MY BLACK HEART.
AND SORRY.

## About the Author

Orli Auslander grew up in London and worked as a milliner and radio DJ in New York City before devoting herself full-time to creating art. Her work has been shown in the United States, England, and Spain, and was recently featured on the Showtime series *Happyish*. She is married to the author Shalom Auslander and lives with her family in upstate New York.